A Real WINNER

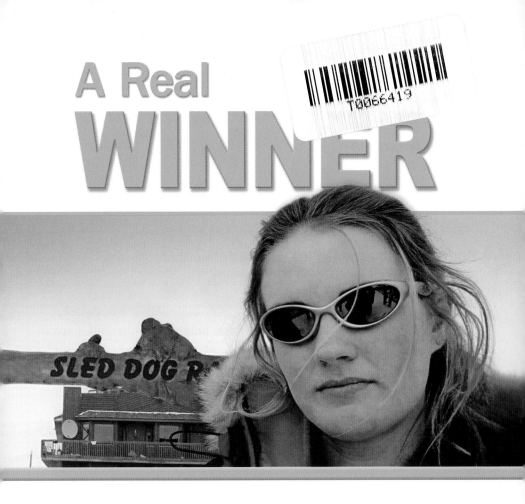

Rob Waring, *Series Editor*

HEINLE
CENGAGE Learning

Australia • Brazil • Japan • Korea • Mexico • Singapore • Spain • United Kingdom • United States

Words to Know

This story is set in the United States. It happens in the state of Oregon, which is in the Cascade [kæskeɪd] Mountains.

A **Dog Sled Racing.** Read the paragraph. Then label the picture with the underlined words.

    Dog sled racing is an exciting sport. In it, dog sledders compete, or 'race,' to be the first person to reach the finish line on a sled. Each sled is pulled by a team of 12 dogs that are tied together with ropes. The person who controls the sled and team is called the musher. Dog sled competitions can last for many days. During this time, mushers must take good care of their dogs, especially the dogs' paws. If a dog hurts its paw, it can't race very well!

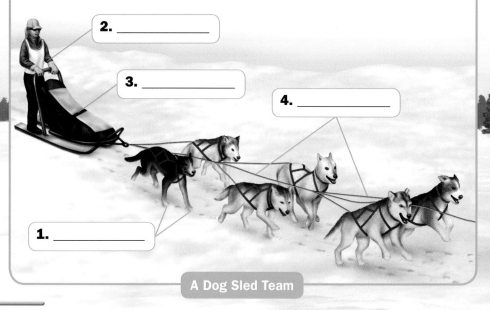

2. _____

3. _____

4. _____

1. _____

A Dog Sled Team

B **A Very Special Racer.** Read the paragraph. Then match each word with the correct definition.

Dog sledding can be a difficult sport, especially if the musher has a disability. In this story, the musher is a young girl who is legally blind. Rachael Scdoris [sədɔrɪs] can see only shapes without clear form or color. Because she can't see, she checks her dogs' ropes by touch. She uses her hands to pet the dogs and encourage them. She also listens carefully to understand her dogs' feelings when they bark. Dog sled races often consist of several legs that the teams run over several days. Because of this, Rachael has a helper who completes the race with her on a snowmobile.

1. disability _____	**a.** touch something gently out of love or caring
	b. make a loud, sharp noise
2. legally blind _____	**c.** unable to see clearly; only able to see light
3. pet _____	**d.** a vehicle with an engine that moves over snow
4. bark _____	**e.** one particular stage or section of an activity
5. leg _____	**f.** something that takes away a mental or physical ability such as hearing or sight
6. snowmobile _____	

a snowmobile

It's winter in the Cascade Mountains of the northwestern United States. Most of 16-year-old Rachael Scdoris' classmates are getting ready for a high school dance, but Rachael has different plans. She's in the process of leading her team of 12 dogs through one of the more difficult dog sled races around—the 'Atta Boy 300' race. The Atta Boy is a staged race that lasts for seven days and goes through the Cascade Mountains. It is divided into seven timed legs, or sections, that total 300 **miles**.[1]

It's early morning on day five of the race. Rachael is getting ready for a long 35-mile run through the mountains. Being a dog sled competitor would be difficult enough for any 16-year-old. However, it's an even bigger challenge for Rachael. Rachael is legally blind.

----

[1]**mile:** 1 mile = 1.61 kilometers

 CD 2, Track 07

The race for this leg of the competition starts. "Three, two, one, go!" says the race official, and Rachael is off for her fifth demanding day of racing. How does a blind girl do this very difficult sport? Jerry Scdoris, Rachael's father, thinks that it's all about his daughter's character. "Rachael never gives up," he explains. "She always **accomplishes**[2] her goals and she works hard at them. That's an **inspiration**[3] to me as a dad."

Jerry, who created the Atta Boy 300 race, is a **world-class champion**[4] in dog sledding. He taught Rachael to 'mush,' or drive a dog sled, when she was only three. She started competing at age 11 and now, at age 16, she is competing in international events. She often races against some of the top competitors in the sport.

---

[2] **accomplish:** finish something successfully or achieve something
[3] **inspiration:** an example which people like and respect
[4] **world-class champion:** the best among the top competitors in the world

Why is 'mushing' so much fun for this 16-year-old? During one of the breaks in the race, Rachael explains, "I've always loved dogs and I've always had a great time running them, and I'm very competitive! So, once I ran all of the local races around here and placed pretty high— or won most of them—it was like, 'Okay, let's move on to the next level.'"

Rachael has been legally blind since birth. What she sees is a world of unclear shapes without form or color. She can't see beyond her lead dog. So how does she manage to race? More importantly, what does she do if there's trouble?

In order to 'mush' well, Rachael depends a lot on her other senses, including her sense of touch. The dogs on her sled team are tied together with special ropes. During a race, these ropes can become **tangled**[5]—and that's exactly what happens to Rachael later in the Atta Boy 300 race!

Eventually, she has to stop and follow the ropes with her hands. She tries to get them straight by touch alone. This time, her hands aren't enough, so Rachael gets her helper, Matt, to assist her. During the race, Matt has traveled along with Rachael on a snowmobile. After he helps her to move the dogs into position, she is able to continue the race.

---

[5]**tangled:** not straight; mixed up

When the ropes become tangled, Rachael must get them straight by touch alone.

Identify Cause and Effect

Circle the cause and underline the effect in each of the sentences.

1. The ropes were tangled so Rachael had to stop.

2. Matt came to assist Rachael because she was having trouble.

3. Rachael was able to finish the race because Matt helped her.

Later, Rachael reflects on the difficulties she had. "I think the hardest part was just keeping it together," she says. "[I was] just thinking, 'Okay, either **quit**[6] right now and stay in the cold, or finish this leg and then do this again tomorrow.'" Rachael decided to continue the race, but unfortunately, she was last across the finish line for the day's leg. Day five of the race was difficult for Rachael, but at least she made it!

---

[6] **quit:** stop; end something

Infer Meaning

1. What does Rachael mean by 'keeping it together'?

2. What does the writer mean by 'made it'?

The next morning it's snowing, but Rachael still has a lot to do. Tonight, she will **camp**[7] with her dogs in the woods before finishing the race tomorrow. She must carefully pack her sled with all the supplies she will need. Rachael's friends and family help her to check and re-check her sled and equipment.

Later that morning, race organizers go over a map of the course. It's a map that Rachael cannot see. She'll rely on her dogs to follow the way. She'll also have Matt close by on his snowmobile if she needs help.

---

[7]**camp:** sleep or stay for a short time in a temporary structure such as a tent

Day six of the race is a leg that covers a total of 43 miles. Just before she starts, Rachael stops to pet and encourage each member of her dog team. She knows that each one of them has a difficult job to do, so they're her primary concern.

Finally, the race starts for the day. The weather is not great, but this leg of the race is going better than yesterday for Rachael. However, there are many difficult turns in the course. Matt has to use his radio to warn Rachael about them several times during the day.

Rachael gets radio messages that tell her what's ahead.

Matt has not worked with Rachael before, but he's impressed with what he's seen. He talks about his time with Rachael: "This is actually my first race with Rachael. So, it's been fun. Mostly I spend the day two miles ahead just kind of **hanging out**.[8] [It] really surprised me … " he adds, "how little Rachael needs my help."

Rachael finishes the sixth leg of the race with a good time for the day. She has moved ahead in the competition, but there's only one more day in the race.

---

[8]**hang out:** wait; do nothing; relax

After a night of camping, Rachael's up very early to examine her dogs before the race. Because she can't see if they've hurt themselves, she has to carefully feel their paws. As she does this, she searches for cuts and **bruises**[9] on them. Gently, she takes care of the dogs and makes sure that each one can run.

Rachael's father notices that his daughter watches every detail carefully so that she can reach her goal. "She's worked so hard for everything that she has … " he says, "and she has just not let anything **deter**[10] her from her goals."

---

[9]**bruise:** a dark area on the skin where one has been hurt
[10]**deter:** stop; turn something or someone away from

Fact Check: True or false?

1. Matt has to help Rachael a lot.

2. Matt communicates with her by telephone.

3. Rachael and her dogs spend the night
   in the woods.

4. Rachael's father feels the dogs' paws.

Finally, it's the last day of the race, and once more Rachael prepares for the long day ahead. This time, she has something special: a group of young fans is **cheering her on**.[11]

Today should be another good run for Rachael. It's a clear winter's day in the beautiful Cascade Mountains. She can't see the wonderful scenery, but Rachael can smell the fresh pine trees. She can also feel the snow and hear the excited barking of her dogs.

---

[11]**cheer (someone) on:** shout loudly to encourage someone

Rachael has a lot of young fans. Does she think of herself as a role model, or someone they can respect? Rachael says: "I don't really consider myself [to be] a role model. If someone wants to think of me as one, that's great. But I don't really see why they would. I expected to come here, do my best, have my dogs do their best, and hopefully finish in the top 15 or 20. But that **obviously**[12] didn't happen. The worst thing you can do is to give up. It doesn't matter what your … 'disability' is, you can **overcome**[13] it."

---

[12] **obvious:** clear; easy to see or understand
[13] **overcome:** succeed in controlling
a problem or challenge

Rachael manages to complete the race. As she passes the finish line, everybody cheers. She finishes the week-long race as the 23rd racer out of 27 racers. Many people are very proud of her and what she has done. She's achieved a lot.

After the race, Rachael stands proudly at the finish line with the other racers. Although she didn't win the race itself, she successfully completed seven days of hard racing. She made it across 300 difficult miles guided by her alternate senses and her love of racing. In many people's opinions, this is what makes Rachael a real winner!

After You Read

1. How many days will Rachael race in the Cascade Mountains?
   A. twelve
   B. seven
   C. thirty-five
   D. five

2. In paragraph 1 on page 6, the word 'demanding' can be replaced by:
   A. distinct
   B. exciting
   C. competitive
   D. difficult

3. According to Rachael, she enjoys racing because she likes to:
   A. show that blind people can do anything
   B. be near the dogs she loves
   C. challenge herself to do better
   D. show that teenagers can run dogs

4. What problem does Rachael face on page 10?
   A. She cannot touch the special ropes.
   B. She must move a dog.
   C. Her assistant slows her down.
   D. She must stop to fix tangled ropes.

5. What's the writer's purpose on page 12?
   A. to show Rachael's strength
   B. to show Rachael's skill
   C. to show that Rachael lost the race
   D. to show Rachael's weakness

6. What is a good heading for page 15?
   A. Dog Sledder Slowed by Rain
   B. Matt Teaches Rachael the Way
   C. Morning Preparation Takes Time
   D. Rachael Does All the Checking

7. In paragraph 1 on page 16, 'them' refers to the:
  A. legs
  B. dogs
  C. number of miles
  D. number of days

8. Matt would probably NOT characterize Rachael as:
  A. weak
  B. confident
  C. skilled
  D. independent

9. In paragraph 2 on page 20, what does 'notices' mean?
  A. hears
  B. is aware of
  C. shares
  D. doesn't care about

10. As she is racing, Rachael can:
  A. feel the snow
  B. smell the trees
  C. listen to her dogs
  D. All of the above.

11. Why does Rachael consider herself to be a good role model?
  A. because she is only sixteen years old
  B. because she always does her best
  C. because she has a disability
  D. She doesn't consider herself to be a role model.

12. What is the writer's opinion of Rachael on page 26?
  A. She will win the next race.
  B. She has achieved a lot.
  C. She should be more competitive.
  D. Her father is proud of her.

What is the Iditarod?

The Iditarod is the world's longest dog sled race. It takes place in Alaska each spring. The course runs from Anchorage to Nome and covers more than 1,000 miles. The race features below-zero temperatures, heavy snow, and several tall mountains. It lasts from ten to twenty days, depending on how fast the teams can travel. Each leg of the race covers from 30 to 50 miles. The name 'Iditarod' originally comes from a Native American word meaning 'a faraway place.'

HOW DID THE RACE START?

In the past, some towns in northern Alaska were hard to reach in winter. People could only get there by taking a dog sled on the Iditarod Trail. The original Iditarod Trail is a series of roads near the Iditarod River in northern Alaska. As the years passed, airplanes and snowmobiles replaced dog teams, and people began to forget about the trail.

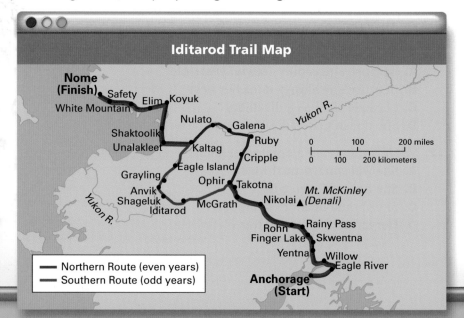

Iditarod Trail Map

Nome (Finish), Safety, White Mountain, Elim, Koyuk, Nulato, Galena, Yukon R., Ruby, Shaktoolik, Unalakleet, Kaltag, Cripple, Eagle Island, Grayling, Ophir, Takotna, Anvik, Shageluk, McGrath, Nikolai, Mt. McKinley (Denali), Iditarod, Rohn, Rainy Pass, Finger Lake, Skwentna, Yentna, Willow, Eagle River, Anchorage (Start), Yukon R.

0 100 200 miles
0 100 200 kilometers

— Northern Route (even years)
— Southern Route (odd years)

Yentna Checkpoint Record

Race Position	Musher	Date & Time In	No. Dogs In	Date & Time Out	No. Dogs Out	Rest Time	Total Time Racing
1	Roger Martin	03/14 12:04	11	03/14 12:17	10	0 h 13 m	7 h 42 m
2	James Brennan	03/14 12:08	11	03/14 12:24	11	0 h 16 m	7 h 53 m
3	Lisa Banks	03/14 12:12	10	03/14 12:25	9	0 h 13 m	7 h 59 m

In 1973, a group of people who were interested in Alaska's history started the race. They didn't want people to forget this important tradition.

HOW DOES A DOG SLED TEAM RUN THE RACE?

Each sled weighs about 40 pounds and carries 100 pounds of food and supplies. It can travel up to 30 miles per hour. The musher starts with a team of 12 to 16 dogs. During the race, some dogs get hurt or become very tired. When this happens, the musher takes the dog out of the race. This is called 'dropping a dog.' Most mushers finish the race with a team of eight dogs.

WHAT ARE SOME OF THE RULES AND REGULATIONS?

- Each dog team must take two 8-hour rest stops and one 24-hour reststop during the race.
- The musher must carry eight sets of special cold-weather shoes called 'booties' for each dog on the team.
- Mushers must stop at each of the 25 checkpoints along the course. A record is created after each checkpoint which reports who is winning and gives further information.

CD 2, Track 08

Word Count: 346
Time: _____

Vocabulary List

accomplish (6)
bark (3, 23)
bruise (20)
camp (15, 20)
cheer (someone) on (23)
deter (20)
disability (3, 24)
hang out (19)
inspiration (6)
leg (3, 4, 6, 10, 12, 16, 19)
legally blind (3, 4, 9)
mile (4, 16, 19, 26)
mush (2, 3, 6, 9, 10)
obvious (24)
overcome (24)
paw (2, 20, 21)
pet (3, 16)
quit (12)
rope (2, 3, 10, 11)
sled (2, 4, 6, 10, 15)
snowmobile (3, 10, 15)
tangle (10, 11)
world-class champion (6)